OUR WORLD OUR FUTURE

Managing the Land

Sharon Dalgleish

CHELSEA HOUSE
PUBLISHERS

A Haights Cross Communications ◆ Company

Philadelphia

Chelsea House Publishers
1974 Sproul Road, Suite 400
Broomall, PA 19008-0914

The Chelsea House world wide web address is www.chelseahouse.com

Library of Congress Cataloging-in-Publication Data

Dalgleish, Sharon.
    Managing the land / by Sharon Dalgleish.

        p. cm. — (Our world: our future)

    Summary: Describes the geological makeup of Earth and the ecosystems it supports; discusses issues
    that affect the land, including population growth, mining, landfills, pollution, erosion; and explains
    how people can help manage and preserve land.

    Includes index.

    ISBN 0-7910-7020-4

    1. Land use—Planning—Juvenile literature. 2. Land tenure—Planning—Juvenile literature. 3. Land use—
    Environmental aspects—Juvenile literature. 4. Urbanization—Juvenile literature. 5. Sustainable
    development—Planning—Juvenile literature. 6. Environmental management—Juvenile literature.
    [1. Land use. 2. Land tenure. 3. Urbanization. 4. Environmental protection.] I. Title.
    II. Our world: our future (Philadelphia, Pa.)

    HD156 .D35 2003

    333.73—dc21

                                                                                    2002002534

First published in 2002 by
MACMILLAN EDUCATION AUSTRALIA PTY LTD
627 Chapel Street, South Yarra, Australia, 3141

Copyright © Sharon Dalgleish 2002
Copyright in photographs © individual photographers as credited

Edited by Sally Woollett
Text design by Karen Young
Cover design by Karen Young
Page layout and simple diagrams by Nina Sanadze
Technical illustrations and maps by Pat Kermode, Purple Rabbit Productions

Printed in China

Acknowledgements
Cover photograph: Llamas at Chimborazo Mountain in Ecuador courtesy of Victor Englebert.

Alcoa World Alumina Australia, p. 8 (top left); Australian Picture Library/Corbis, pp. 13, 14, 16,
18 (bottom), 21 (bottom), 23 (top), 25 (bottom); Australian Picture Library/Vandystaadt, p. 22 (left);
Coo-ee Picture Library, pp. 8 (top right), 12 (bottom); The DW Stock Picture Library, pp. 4 (top left, top
center, top right and bottom), 6, 11; Victor Englebert, pp. 7 (desert), (grassland), 10 (top), 24 (bottom);
Getty Images/Photodisc, pp. 4 (bottom center), 10 (bottom), 12 (top), 18 (top), 25, 30; Imageaddict.com,
pp. 4 (bottom right), 8 (bottom left); Fred Adler/Kino Archives, pp. 15 (right), 19, 21 (top); Legend Images,
pp. 8 (center and bottom right), 17 (bottom), 29; Dr Stuart Miller/Lochman Transparencies, pp. 22 (right),
28; Stewart Roper/Lochman Transparencies, p. 24 (top); photolibrary.com, p. 7 (Arctic); Southern Images/
Silkstone, pp. 7 (evergreen forest), 15 (left), 23 (bottom); Ron Giling/Still Pictures, p. 28; Rob Blakers/
Tasmanian Photo Library, p. 7 (rainforest); VISY Recycling, p. 17 (top); World Images, p. 7 (mountains).

While every care has been taken to trace and acknowledge copyright, the publisher tenders their apologies for
any accidental infringement where copyright has proved untraceable.

Contents

READ
MORE ABOUT:

Look out for this
box. It will tell
you the other
pages in this book
where you can find
out more about
related topics.

Our world

 OUR WORLD

We are connected to everything in our world. We are connected through the air we breathe, the water we drink, the food we eat, the energy we use, and the soil we live on.

To keep our world healthy, all these elements must work together.

water

land

energy

wildlife

forests

air

SHOW ME

The parts of your body work together to keep you healthy. If one part of your body stops working properly, you get sick!

Our future

The number of people in our world is now doubling every 40 years. This means that when you are grown up there could be twice as many people on Earth as there are now.

Every person on Earth needs certain things to survive. We need to make sure our world will still be able to give people everything they need to live, now and in the future.

▲ Now.

▲ Forty years from now.

STOP & THINK

Suppose that one part of our world were to stop working properly. What do you think might happen to the rest of our world?

To the center of Earth

Earth is shaped like a big ball. Inside the ball there are layers made of different materials. It is a bit like a hard-boiled egg! We live on the outside—on the thin shell called the crust.

The crust is made of rocks. The rocks are in layers built up over millions of years. Oceans cover most of Earth's crust. The part of the crust that is above the water is called land.

Earth has a mass of about 6,000,000,000,000, 000,000,000,000, kilograms!

▼ Earth is made up of layers.

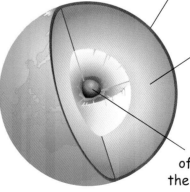

The crust is made up of rocks. It is up to 50 miles (80 kilometers) thick under mountains but much thinner under some parts of the ocean.

The mantle is made up of hot rock. It is 1,700 miles (3,000 kilometers) thick.

The core is made of metal. It is solid on the inside and thick liquid metal on the outside.

▲ If you look carefully at this cliff face, you can see how the crust is made up of layers of rock.

SHOW ME

Earth is not a perfect ball shape. It is more like the shape of an orange—a bit fatter than it is tall. If Earth were the same size as an apple, the crust would be thinner than the skin on the apple.

Sharing the land

Only about one-third of Earth's surface is land. People must share this land with plants and animals. The land supports an amazing number of environments.

hot deserts	windy mountains	rainforests	grassland	evergreen forests	freezing Arctic and Antarctic regions

Each of these environments is called an ecosystem. In an ecosystem, the land, plants and animals all work in harmony and balance. Changing one part of an ecosystem affects every other part. Changing the land will change other parts of the environment.

STOP & THINK

How can we make sure these ecosystems (including our own) keep working in harmony and balance?

7

Living off the land

The land provides almost everything we need. It gives us food to keep our bodies healthy, **fossil fuels** to power our machines, and **raw materials**, such as metal, stone and wood, to make things. We build our homes on it. We use it for leisure. We even argue over who owns it.

Look at all the things in the room you are in right now. Can you work out how they all had their beginnings in the land?

▲ Aluminum comes from a red rock (bauxite) stripped from Earth's crust.

▲ Rubber is produced from a tree grown in the soil.

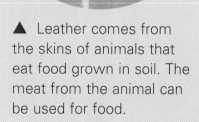

▲ Leather comes from the skins of animals that eat food grown in soil. The meat from the animal can be used for food.

▲ Plastic is made from oil or coal mined from Earth's crust.

STOP & THINK
Will the land be able to provide everything we need in the future?

▲ Concrete is a mixture of clay, limestone and sand dug from Earth's crust.

Handle with care

The land is made of rocks, sand and soil. Soil is made out of broken-up pieces of rock, dead leaves, tree branches and dead bugs! It can take 1,000 years for rock to break down to form about 1 inch (2 to 3 centimeters) of soil. If people grew that slowly it would take almost 80,000 years for them to grow up!

Soil is hard to make but easy to damage. People damage the soil by:

• farming, which adds chemicals to the land and can cause soil erosion

• mining, which scars the land and creates waste that can poison the soil

• cutting down forests, which causes soil erosion

• building over the natural land.

We need to look after this thin layer of soil. Otherwise, it will be unable to provide for people in the future.

1 Dead matter breaks down to keep the topsoil healthy.

2 Topsoil is alive with roots, tiny bacteria and worms. Air and water fill any spaces.

3 Harder material is difficult for the plant roots to get through.

4 Parent material is the rock and soil that breaks up to form the other layers.

▲ Soil is alive!

READ MORE ABOUT:

• soil erosion on page 10

• building on the land on page 12

• mining the land on page 14.

SHOW ME

Imagine a giant tomato as big as a seven-story building. Now imagine that the giant tomato is Earth. The soil on top would be far thinner than the skin of a normal-sized tomato.

Wanted! More soil for food

The number of people living in our world is growing by 90 million people a year. To feed all these hungry people, we need more and more land to grow food. A lot of this food is produced on huge farms, where farmers try to grow as much as they can as quickly as they can.

To make room for more farmland, forests have to be cut down. Farm animals break up the soil with their hooves. The soil can easily be swept away by wind and rain, because there are no longer any large tree roots to hold it together and no blanket of fallen leaves to cover it. This is called soil erosion.

If farmers are not careful about the methods they use, the soil loses its rich goodness. Soon it cannot be used to grow anything. In the worst cases, it turns into desert. If farming methods continue to destroy the land in this way, there will be no land left for farming in the future.

▲ This land in Colombia was once covered in forest. The forest was cut down to make room for more farmland.

▶ In the United States, most of the soil lost each year is because of damage by farm animals.

STOP & THINK

Can we feed our growing population and keep the soil healthy to grow food in the future?

Saving soil

If we are to grow more and more food on the same amount of land, we need to look after that land very carefully.

Working out the best way to farm is tricky. Every area is part of an ecosystem where soil, plants, animals and weather are connected in their own way. But improving our methods of farming is worth it for our world.

One way to help stop soil erosion is to plant trees among farm crops. The trees' roots hold onto the soil, and the trunk and leafy branches stop the wind from blowing the soil away. On hills and mountains, farmers can cut terraces into the slope. This keeps rainwater from washing the soil away down the slope.

▲ Planting a row of trees beside a field reduces soil erosion.

YOU CAN DO iT!

❀ If you live on a farm, plant trees to make sure your soil stays where it is.

❀ If you have a garden, grow your own vegetables.

❀ Start a compost pile.

❀ Eat less meat. Farm animals, such as cattle, cause a lot of damage to the soil.

OUR WORLD

Creeping concrete jungles

More than half of all the people in our world live in cities. These cities cover twice as much land today as they did 20 years ago. Cities have spread over land once used to grow food. Land that was once covered in forests is now paved in concrete.

In 1950 there were 50 million cars and trucks in our world. Today there are 500 million. One hundred thousand new cars are made every day. If we did not have so many cars, we would not need so many roads.

Cities use huge amounts of water. A lot of the water they use is supplied by **reservoirs** made by building a dam across a river. When a reservoir is created, large areas of land are flooded. Huge areas of farmland and rainforest have been lost in this way.

▲ Freeways and main roads make it easier for cities to spread out. Then the roads take up even more land.

▶ This land used to be covered in forest before it was flooded to make a reservoir.

STOP & THINK

How will people be able to grow food in the future if we have paved over or flooded all the land?

Planning better cities

There is a way that people can live in cities without destroying the land. All it takes is planning! How does your nearest city score on the well-planned city checklist?

The city of New York used so much water that a giant new dam was needed. Instead of building the dam, the water company replaced over one million toilets in the city with toilets that used less water. It cost more than $250 million, but it was cheaper than building the new reservoir—and it saved the land from being flooded.

CHECKLIST FOR A WELL-PLANNED CiTY!

PUBLiC TRANSPORTATiON
☐ Is it cheap and well organized?
A good public transportation system means fewer cars and fewer roads.

SEWAGE
☐ Is it treated and used to fertilize parks and green spaces?
Reusing water means we do not have to flood the land to make more reservoirs.

HOUSEHOLD TRASH
☐ Is it all recycled or composted?
If we produce less garbage, we will not use up so much land space to store it.

◀ These people are protesting about the building of a new road. They want to save the natural land.

YOU CAN DO iT!

❀ Save water so we do not need to build so many, or such large, dams. Here are some ways you can do it:

❀ Remind your parents to fix leaky faucets.

❀ Do not take long showers.

❀ If you prefer to soak in the tub, fill it only halfway.

❀ Turn off the faucet while you brush your teeth.

❀ Whenever you can, walk instead of taking a car. That way we will not need so many new roads!

READ MORE ABOUT:

• recycling on page 17.

13

Digging it up

The land's resources—the raw materials we use to make other things—are held in the rock and soil. To get the resources, we have to dig them out of a quarry or mine. As a mine or quarry grows, it creates huge piles of waste. More and more land has to be cleared to store the waste.

Mining and quarrying

1 A space is cleared for the mine or quarry.

2 Roads are built so material mined can be taken away.

3 Machines dig up the ground and the resource is taken away.

4 Waste material and wastewater created is disposed of.

5 The land is cleaned up when the mine or quarry is finished.

▲ Bingham Canyon copper mine in the United States is 750 yards (700 meters) deep. It covers an area of more than 16,000 basketball courts. Since 1906 more than 5.5 billion tons (5 billion metric tons) of rock have been removed, and the mine is still growing.

• **In the United States, mining creates 4.5 billion tons (4 billion metric tons) of waste each year.**

• **In the United States, each person uses 21 tons (19 metric tons) of minerals every year. This does not include fossil fuels used for energy!**

The big growth in the number of people in our world has meant a big growth in the demand for resources. **Developing countries** once used only a small amount of resources. Now they are using more. Some resources that it takes nature millions of years to make might soon run out. If we use them up they will be gone forever.

STOP & THINK

Will there be any resources left for people in the future to use?

Digging with care

Raw materials from the land are made into all kinds of useful things. We do not want to live without them. If we are careful and use the raw materials wisely, there will be enough left for people in the future.

It is not possible to leave the ground untouched if we want to reach the resources. But we can treat the land with care and repair the damage caused. Some countries have strict rules that a mining site must be put back to its natural state after a mine is finished. This costs the mining company a lot of money. Some mining companies have moved to poorer, developing countries where the rules are not so strict. Is it fair to scar and poison someone else's land?

▼ This land has been ruined by careless mining. Nothing can live here. The scar will remain for hundreds of years.

◄ This land used to be a mining site. It has been successfully restored as a public garden.

YOU CAN DO IT!

❀ Before you buy something, think about where the raw materials to make it came from. Do you really need to buy it? Only buy it if the answer is "yes."

❀ Try not to buy things that are meant to be thrown away, such as disposable cameras or paper plates. Buy high-quality products and keep them for a lifetime—this way fewer raw materials will be dug from the land.

❀ Try to buy things only in containers that can be reused or refilled.

READ MORE ABOUT:

• raw materials from the land on page 8.

15

Mountains made of garbage

Most of the garbage we throw away ends up buried in landfills. Landfills are big holes in the land where garbage is compressed and covered in soil.

This is what an average person in a **developed country** throws away every year. How much do you throw away?

- 100 aluminum drink cans
- 100 glass bottles or jars
- 110 pounds (50 kilograms) of plastic
- 70 steel cans
- a few big trees worth of paper
- 330 pounds (150 kilograms) of food scraps

North Americans are the biggest producers of garbage in the world. About 110 million tons (100 million metric tons) of garbage are produced every day in the United States. This uses up a lot of space!

Australians are the second biggest producers of garbage. About 230,000 shopping bags are dumped in landfills every hour. Only a tiny number of these bags are recycled. Yet plastic bags are made from oil, a fossil fuel that could run out in 40 years. The amount of oil used to make one plastic bag would fuel a car for about 35 feet (11 meters).

▲ The huge mound behind these houses is Fresh Kills landfill in Staten Island, New York. It is so big that it can be seen from space.

STOP & THINK

How can we keep our world from being covered in mountains of garbage?

Use up the land or use it again?

Garbage in landfills takes a long time to rot away. Whole hotdogs have been found in landfills ten years after they were dumped. Plastics can take 200 to 400 years to break down. Some do not break down at all.

The glass, plastic, metal, paper and cloth we throw away in landfills could all be recycled. Most of the food scraps (not meat) could also be recycled as compost for gardens and green spaces. It just takes a bit of planning and effort.

▶ Using food scraps to make compost solves two problems at once. Less land is taken up with garbage, and the soil is kept healthy.

▲ Paper recycling plants save raw materials, so we do not need to take so much from the land. Less garbage also means fewer landfills will be needed.

YOU CAN DO IT!

❀ Nearly one-third of garbage in landfills in developed countries is packaging. Do not buy anything that has too much packaging.

❀ Reuse glass bottles and jars. If you cannot reuse them, take them to be recycled.

❀ Reuse old plastic containers. Use them as storage boxes, for growing plants or mixing paint.

❀ Try not to use plastic shopping bags. Take your own canvas bag or backpack. If you must use a plastic bag, save it to use again next time or reuse it as a garbage can liner.

❀ Do not throw fruit and vegetable peelings in the trash to end up in landfills. Make compost with them and then spread it on the soil.

READ MORE ABOUT:

• materials that do not break down on page 18

• making compost on page 27.

Poisoning the land

▼ The pollution coming out of this factory smokestack is being released into the air.

Mines, factories, power stations and cars produce chemicals that can harm the land. The chemicals can remain and be dangerous for hundreds, or even thousands, of years.

The wastes and chemicals that do not break down in nature are the most dangerous. This means they may stay in the soil and poison it. Some chemicals pumped into the air can mix with water and turn into **acid**. This acid falls to the ground and poisons the soil.

In 1986 there was an explosion in the nuclear power station at Chernobyl in Ukraine. Clouds of **radiation** spread into the air. The clouds drifted over Europe, poisoning land and crops growing in the soil. The land near Chernobyl still cannot be used or lived on today.

Chemicals are also used for farming. Farmers use **fertilizers** to make crops grow. They use **pesticides** to keep crops from being eaten by insects. These chemicals can pollute the soil and can kill the bacteria, worms and other **decomposers** that make new soil.

◀ No one can live near Chernobyl because the land is **contaminated**.

STOP & THINK
Can we reduce the amount of dangerous chemicals we produce?

Safer waste

More than 440 million tons (400 million metric tons) of poisonous waste is produced in our world every year. Some countries now have laws to force companies to safely get rid of waste.

> Just about all the food you eat comes from the land. (All except the food that grows in the sea!) It was all once a living plant that grew in the soil, or a living animal that ate a plant that grew in the soil. If we poison the soil, we poison ourselves.

Waste from nuclear power stations stays dangerous for thousands of years. Some waste is made into a kind of glass, poured into steel tanks, sealed in concrete and buried deep in the ground. Other waste is stored in barrels. Scientists are thinking about ways to make the waste safer.

Some farmers grow food without using harmful chemicals. They use **compost** and animal manure to feed their crops. This kind of farming is called organic farming.

▲ Some shops specialize in selling organic fruit and vegetables. They may not look as good as those grown with chemicals, but they are better for the land.

YOU CAN DO IT!

- ❀ Do not buy products made by companies that dump poisonous waste.
- ❀ Recycle as much as you can. If there is less waste to deal with overall we will have more time and resources to work out ways of dealing with dangerous waste.
- ❀ Power stations produce pollution that makes acid rain, so do not waste electricity.
- ❀ Cars produce pollution that makes acid rain, so use your feet instead of the car.
- ❀ Tell your parents not to use weed killers in the garden. Weed by hand!

Global warming and the land

Some of the gases in our world's atmosphere act like a sheet of glass on a greenhouse. They let the sunlight through but do not let all the heat back out—just like inside a real greenhouse. This greenhouse effect keeps Earth much warmer than it would otherwise be. Without it, our world would be covered in ice.

Power stations, factories and cars are pumping too many greenhouse gases into our world's atmosphere. This traps too much heat, and our world gets even warmer. Scientists call this gradual warming of our whole world global warming.

As our world gets warmer, so does the sea. Warm water takes up more space than cold water. As the sea takes up more space, the sea levels rise. The sea level has risen about 8 inches (20 centimeters) in the last 100 years.

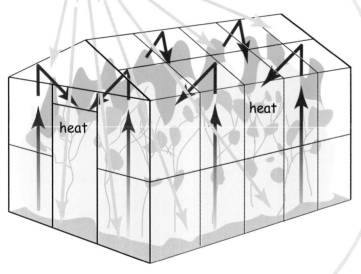

Sun

heat

heat

▲ Greenhouses are used mainly in cold countries. The heat trapped inside helps the flowers and vegetables grow.

STOP & THINK
What happens to the land when we pump extra greenhouse gases into the atmosphere?

Floods and droughts

Global warming could cause the land in some parts of the world to disappear under water. In other places, land may dry up.

People living on some of the islands in the South Pacific are already noticing the effects of rising sea levels. The rising water level is taking over land that was once used for farming. The seawater is making other parts of the land too salty to farm and is causing erosion. The residents of the islands may soon need somewhere else to live.

If the climate changes, about half the land in our world will probably become drier. This land will no longer be suitable for farming because there will not be enough water.

▲ If the sea continues to rise, a quarter of Bangladesh will disappear under water.

◄ The land in dry grassland areas, such as the Texas Great Plains, will become too dry for crops or cattle.

YOU CAN DO IT!

❀ Plant a tree. Trees take in carbon dioxide (a greenhouse gas) and give out clean oxygen for us to breathe.

❀ Most electricity is made by burning fossil fuels, which release greenhouse gases. So save as much electricity as you can around the house. Here are some ways you can do it:

❀ Turn lights off when you leave the room.

❀ Turn down the heat. If you are cold, put on more clothes.

❀ Cars run on fossil fuels, so do not ask your parents to drive you places when you could easily and safely walk.

READ MORE ABOUT:

• soil erosion on page 10.

Getting away from it all

Most of us will never see land that has not been touched by people. Yet many of us would like to. Visiting our world's wonders and natural places is more popular than ever. In the United States today, 12 times more people visit national parks than visited them in 1950.

The vacation business is growing so fast that one in every ten people in our world works in **tourism**. Some people think this number will double in the next ten years.

People who visit wilderness areas can easily damage the land. The natural environment can be disturbed easily if we do not manage it carefully.

▲ People like to climb Mount Everest, but look at the garbage some of them leave behind. It will not break down, and so it will blow around the mountain for hundreds of years.

STOP & THINK

How can we manage tourism so that the land is left undamaged for people in the future?

▲ These tourists are photographing a penguin colony in Antarctica. In 1990 only a few hundred tourists visited Antarctica. In 1996 there were more than 10,000 tourists.

Antarctica has been called the last great wilderness area. Some people think all tourism to Antarctica should be banned because it is the last area of unspoiled wilderness and the land is too easily damaged.

Learning about the land

OUR FUTURE

If tourism is not managed well, it can be just as damaging to the land as mining or using harmful farming techniques. But managing it well allows people to learn about the environment and to enjoy its natural beauty.

Some wilderness areas have not been changed by people. They are now often protected by law. However, many people want to travel to places of great natural beauty. Governments are now trying to protect certain wilderness areas while still allowing visitors. This type of tourism is called ecotourism. Ecotourism can also help people learn about the land so they can better care for our world.

We need to control tourism so that both the land and the people living on it can benefit. There must be a balance between attracting travelers and looking after the land.

Subtidal seagrasses

In deeper water, below the low tide level, there are beds of larger seagrasses. These expansive marine meadows are notable as habitat for fish, crabs and dophins. The death of seagrasses reduces the available habitat for these animals and leads to sand drift, which may then damage other environments.

▲ These children are on a swamp trail in the Florida Everglades. Education helps make people aware of the land and how to look after it.

◀ Many parks and reserves have educational displays to teach people about the land.

YOU CAN DO IT!

❋ If you go on vacation, walk or rent a bicycle instead of using a car.

❋ If you go on vacation, do not leave litter behind to pollute the land.

❋ Find out all you can about a place you are visiting. If you understand the land, you can look after it—and even help protect it.

❋ If you go walking or climbing in natural places, stay on the paths and obey any signs so you do not do any damage.

23

Sacred land

Many early people around the world thought of Earth as a mother—as the one who gave life to everything. They often called the land Mother Earth. They believed that Earth cared for them so they should care for it. Some American Indians would not even dig in Earth. They believed it would mean wounding their mother. To many **indigenous** people today, the land still has spiritual meaning.

The Australian Aboriginal people lived off the land for more than 50,000 years without mining it or farming on it. When European settlers arrived, they claimed the land as their own. The settlers believed that only written documents proved ownership.

Different people have different ideas about the land and how it should be managed. It is not easy for everyone to agree how to manage the land.

▲ Australian Aboriginal people believe that the land is sacred and that each part of it has a spirit. They call the beginning of the world the Dreaming. In the Dreaming, the Ancestors rose from below Earth to change into the land, mountains, rivers, rocks, animals and other parts of nature. Their spirits are still there. Aboriginal people believe humans are part of nature, not separate from it or better than it.

STOP & THINK
Who owns the wilderness?

▲ These Yanomami Indians live in the Amazon rainforest in Brazil. They want to live on their own land in their traditional ways. But settlers, farmers and miners also want to use the land.

Managing the land

The land has different values to different people:

- Farmers need soil to grow crops, so they cut down the trees.

- Loggers want to cut down the trees for timber to build houses and make furniture and paper.

- Miners want to dig the land to get at the raw materials in the rocks below.

- Scientists want to study the animals and plants on the land.

- Environmentalists think some areas should be kept as wilderness.

- Indigenous people see the land as a provider of food, medicine and materials. They also see it as part of their spirit.

When people see the same thing in different ways, it can lead to arguments. Politicians and courts of law have to decide who should own and manage the land.

▲ American Indians have deep respect for the land. Many see it as a sacred resource that needs to be protected.

YOU CAN DO iT!

✿ Get out into nature whenever you have the chance. See how amazing land is—even if it is only in your own backyard.

✿ Try and visit a national park or reserve. Find out if there is anything you can do to help look after it.

✿ If you visit a place, find out all about the land in that place and the indigenous people who live there. Look after the land while you are there and respect the local beliefs and way of life.

READ MORE ABOUT:

• mining the land on page 14.

Create a landfill in the garden

What you need:

- land in a garden or at school (Ask permission first!)

- small garden shovel

- different items of trash, such as apple cores, vegetable peelings, paper, plastic bags, aluminum foil

- stones.

What to do:

1 Dig a hole about 4 to 6 inches (10 to 15 centimeters) deep for each item.

2 Put each item in a separate hole and cover with soil.

3 Use a stone to mark where you buried each item. You could also write a list so you can remember what you buried!

4 Wait one month. Then dig up the items. What has happened to each one? Have any disappeared? Are there any that will not rot?

Be a dirt detective

Fill an empty drink carton with garden soil. (Ask permission to dig if it is not your garden!) Tip the soil onto a piece of newspaper and spread it out. Look for rock, bits of plants or twigs, worms, beetles, ants and other crawly things. If you have a magnifying glass, look through it. Count how many different kinds of things you see. There are even more things you cannot see. One pinch of soil can contain a million fungi and over a billion bacteria.

Make some compost

Stop sending so much trash to landfills—and at the same time, make the soil rich and healthy!

What you need:

- old plastic garbage can with the bottom cut out

- the garbage can lid

- old broomstick

- a corner of the garden

- plenty of garden and kitchen waste— see "What you can use in your compost" for ideas

- gardening gloves.

What to do:

1 Make sure the open bottom of the can is sitting on soil, not on paving.

2 Wearing gardening gloves, break the waste material into small pieces and pile it loosely inside the can. The smaller the pieces, the faster they will compost. Be careful not to breathe in any particles while you are breaking them up.

3 When the trash can is full, poke an old broomstick into it a few times. Make sure you push the stick right to the bottom of the can. This will make holes to let air in.

4 Put the lid on. The waste inside should eventually heat up.

5 Leave your bin for a few months. When the compost is dark and crumbly, it is ready to spread on the garden.

What you can use in your compost:

- coffee grounds, tea leaves and eggshells

- lawn clippings, leaves and twigs

- manure

- paper and thin cardboard

- vacuum-cleaner dust

- fruit and vegetable peelings

- straw and hay.

Think globally

Around our world we are losing treasures from under our feet. We build houses and roads on the land. We use up the goodness in the soil and even change it to desert. We take resources from deep underground and leave scars that will last for hundreds of years. And we pollute the land and soil with our waste.

As the population in our world grows, so too will the demands for land. All countries must work together to manage the land and its resources in a **sustainable** way. We also need international laws to protect areas of wilderness around our world.

United Nations

In December 1996, the United Nations Convention to Combat Desertification came into force. Desertification is a big word for the way good land slowly becomes less and less healthy. Scientists are still learning what causes it and how to treat and prevent it. The Convention encourages countries to share research efforts and action plans. Every country that signed the convention must obey its laws.

▲ Antarctica is the only place left in our world that is almost unchanged by people. But resource treasures lie under the Antarctic ice. In 1991 countries around the world made a **treaty** not to mine it for 50 years. We must use resources wisely so that we never need to begin mining there.

▶ The United Nations works towards international cooperation.

STOP & THINK
What will happen if all countries do not use the land and its resources wisely?

Governments in action

Every year we destroy 25 billion tons (23 billion metric tons) more soil than nature can make. If you loaded this soil onto a train, the train would be long enough to stretch 150 times around Earth.

In 1992 governments from around the world met at an Earth Summit in Brazil. It was the world's biggest meeting. All the leaders at the meeting signed an agreement called Agenda 21. It is a plan for using—and looking after—our world in the 21st century. All countries could do more to keep our world healthy. The strength of Agenda 21 is that the world's leaders agreed that we need to take action.

Agenda 21: Aims for our land

- Look after soil and stop the spread of deserts.

- Improve country living conditions so fewer people move to cities.

- Save resources by reusing materials.

- Make companies that damage or pollute the land pay to clean it up.

- Make sure new tourist resorts and hotels suit the local land.

- Use both modern and traditional methods to manage the land.

▲ The United Kingdom was once covered in forests. Now only a very small part of the land area has trees. The government is working to plant more trees to protect the land.

YOU CAN DO iT!

❀ Write to politicians and tell them what you think needs to be done to wisely manage the land.

❀ Talk to your parents about what you can do at home to help the land and soil.

❀ Check if there are any environmental groups in your area. If there isn't already a group you can join, start one yourself at school.

❀ Organize a recycling center at your school. Do not forget a compost bin for lunchbox scraps!

Sustaining our world

To survive on this planet, we need to take and use the things our world gives us. But we also need to keep all the parts of our world working in balance. Scientists call it ecologically sustainable development. It means taking only what we need from our world to live today, and at the same time keeping our world healthy so it can keep giving in the future.

We must change the way we live. Otherwise all the rich, healthy soil, as well as all the resources hidden in Earth's crust, will be used up. We need to leave enough resources in the land for people to live—today and in the future.

Everything in our world is connected. If we damage one part, we can affect the other parts. And if we look after one part, we can help protect all the other parts. The future of our world depends on our actions now.

▼ The different parts of our world are all connected.

Glossary

acid a chemical that eats away solid material

compost dead plant matter

contaminated dirty or diseased

decomposers living things that break down dead matter

developed country a country where the way of life is based on the use of resources by industries

developing countries countries based on farming that are trying to develop their resources

fertilizers something added to the soil to make plants grow faster or bigger

fossil fuels fuels such as coal or gas that formed in Earth from the remains of animals and plants

indigenous originally living in an area

minerals any solid, non-plant, non-animal materials in nature

pesticides chemicals used to kill plant or animal pests

radiation energy or particles released when uranium breaks down

raw materials materials used to make something else

reservoirs lakes that form behind dams

sewage waste carried away in sewers and drains

sustainable the use of resources in a way that leaves enough for others to use over a long period of time

tourism the business of organizing services for tourists

treaty an agreement between two or more countries

Index